Oceans and Black

All rig

Presentation by *BookLeaf Publishing*

Web: www.bookleafpub.com

E-mail: info@bookleafpub.com

ISBN: 9789358736106

First edition 2023

*To Dad, you scooped me up and loved me
back to life*

Oceans and
Black Holes

Lydia Jones

BookLeaf
Publishing

India | USA | UK

ACKNOWLEDGEMENT

My family, who loved me when I couldn't love myself

Jackie and Bev, guiding lights out of the darkness

KB, a week was all that was needed to discover the poet in me

The rooms, where I found love, acceptance, tolerance and above all laughter

PREFACE

"To see a world in a grain of sand
And a heaven in a wild flower
Hold infinity in the palm of your hand
And eternity in an hour"

- William Blake

An Omen

She is coming, they said
I don't believe you, I said
She's a force, they said
I'm stronger, I said
Watch on the fourth, they said
That's my birthday, I said
It's foretold, they said
Whatever, I said

And when she came, they said
Only four foot tall, I said
Slender frame, they said
The only giveaway, I said
Her fierce red eyes, they said
Demonic or angelic, I said
Hard to tell these days, they said

A Glimpse

The weight of your hand as I held it
Warmth of your arms against me
like you meant it
Expert kisses wake up what's been long buried
Thumbs caress fingers and palms unhurried
Side by side, focused on resisting
My desire to touch you, not on who's speaking
The delicious slow burn
A thrill when your name arrives on my phone
Beneath my eyelids I replay you entering
Evoke your scent to burn me, surrendering

Now I return lonely
To listen only
To songs in the minor key
That promise me one day I'll be free
I'm reluctant to change the sheets,
was I dreaming?
What's awake now, I'll sing her back to sleeping

Yet my heart didn't crack
But it was starting to remember
As we fade to black
We didn't make it to September

A glimpse is all I caught
While you say there's no capacity
For the future that I sought
The darkness that lives inside of me
Will tell me it's not just anybody -
…But just my body
How long until your hand rests in another's?
How fast will you rebuild your heart
To give it willingly to some other?
Because if you had asked
I would have lent it freely
You see my capacity is overflowing
I see what's inside of me
I just have no way of knowing
Where to put
This love I almost felt
That took
Courage and fear
And turned it into a window
I stooped down and peered -
Through to see the light of some potential
Snuffed out to keep confidential
In the confines of my mind
As there's nothing more to see
And my brain chemistry
Will return to balance
As I settle in, once more to silence

New Worlds

Why am I drawn to you?
Like light to a black hole, inescapable
Or better yet, a neutron star
Once glorious now breakable
On its way to a cold death
Creating new worlds
As it draws its last breath

Surely there's a place
Where my heart has not gotten lost
Searching for your face
To beat faster and ignore the costs
A place where I'm not checking everyday
I'm not steadying myself for, say
That inevitable disappointment of finding
another's innocent smile
Just so I can savour the first sip of envy, while
My heart shrinks and hardens
Maybe this world doesn't have an internet at all
Maybe it's been built on star power not
hydrocarbons

And on this new world, maybe
There's a version of you and me
Where our week lasted years

And no excuses appeared
Where my hair goes grey
And you would stay
For us to grow
Together, hands holding, living slow
Laughing at each other's jokes
Bingeing box sets, God bless,
our prayer that evokes
A scnsc of bclonging
That's all I am looking for
All for what I'm longing
And I know it's possible
Somewhere among these dying stars,
even probable

Home Is...

Home is a house
Home is my house
Home is your warmth
Home is not going without
Home is your arms wrapped around cold limbs
Home is a fever that burns from within
Home is laughter
Home is bargaining
Home is staring past her
Home is darkening
Home is climbing the same stairs over and over
Home is belonging
Home is staying sober
Home is lush green stems growing long and
strong with watering
Home is your eyes, deep dark blue, unaltering
Home is falling asleep next to you every night
Home is waking up, cups of tea, your invite
Home is making plans
Home is taking pills
Home is hand in hand
Home is all the frills
Home is mended hearts
Home is listening
Home is friends that part

Home is tears glistening
Home is reading books
Home is eating toast
Home is sideways looks
Home is you I love the most

Lovers

It's been nearly six years
Since my bed has been shared
Slept limbs intertwined
Held from behind
Sleepless nights
Pressed against me tight
Two teas in the morning
Leave for work both yawning

Now I sleep spread out
Both sides of the bed allowed
As if I'm floating on my back
Adrift on the high seas
I don't feel there's a lack
In fact, it's fine, I feel free

I've started to see
A new person recently
We're figuring out if we can be lovers
Before we dive under the covers
We haven't slept together yet
Not that I would object
To letting them into my bed
And welcome sleepless nights instead

Sparks

Tuesday
A middle of the road day
Nothing good or bad to say
Clouds above nothingy and grey
Still jumper weather
Carry an umbrella for good measure

Matthew feels the pressure
From his parents to become a professor
Or lawyer, even better
But he lives for literature
Art and cinema
Sheds tears at gigs of his favourite bands
Writes short stories in cafes by hand

Amy's not especially clever
Mainly motivated by pleasure
Never will she miss Love Island
Summertime she'll bake in sunlight and
Top up her tan
With St Tropez or Molly Mae's brand
Nails and brows always done
Long blonde hair curled or up in a bun

Neither Matt nor Amy have ever been in love

Only twenty-two years old each
They've been distracted by a crush
But never invaded by another, unable to breathe

Amy and Matt live on the same street
In the same building
But they are yet to meet
Until this Tuesday, Matt is filming
Some exterior shots in the local park
Amy's walking her dog, Lemar
They both look up at the exact same moment
Something passes between them quite potent
Amy has met her final lover
Matt is looking at his future kid's mother
Sparks pierce both of their hearts
Sparks that make their mark as lasting as a tattoo
Sparks that turn a dark sky blue
Sparks that say that love is true

What Will Survive Us?

What will survive us
When we're done?
Gone to dust
When God has won
Atoms flying back to the stars
Our Sun's expansion
We can't outrun

What will survive us
When our voices quieten?
Memories fade
Sky darkens
When your stories end
And they grow beyond
Light doesn't bend
Phones won't respond

What will survive us
When the oceans flood?
The cities sink
Empty buildings fall to the mud
Ice sheets spreading
Desert creeps over our blood
Prayers remain unanswered
Insects scatter as if drugged

What will survive us
When the button has been pushed?
Just computer code for AI
Waiting for commands
When we're cooked
The sky blacked out and poisoned
Robots crush skulls underfoot
Vision clouded by noise and
A single preacher
Quoting psalms from a book

What will survive us
When a rock collides?
Sending ash up high
That hides the sky
Our wheat and barley
Flake in the fields
Cows and sheep
Faint hungry then die
Fighting in the streets
Lovers in the sheets
Children running wild
Among the grey concrete

What will survive us
Beyond the last breath?
When our blood has run cold
And we lose all our strength

For the box that contains us
Is burnt with our bones
And the dust that remains just
Scatters so they can go home

What will survive us
When we're done?
When your time has run out
A long sleep has begun
Will we sing songs?
Will we see the one?
Can we hold hands?
Will it be fun?

Road to 11 Billion

Dear Grandad,
I hope you're okay
Mama bought some water today
She had to fight someone
For the last one
So we won't go thirsty
I might be allowed to have some tea
I've been waiting for when it's just you and me
But we now have to save the electricity
So there'll be no visit this month, sorry

School's closed now too
I heard there was a new
Collapsed ice shelf
Perhaps that's why school's flooded?
My teacher says the Chinese can stop it
But Georgie says they won't without a profit
Is that true Grandad?
Could there really be a plan that
Includes us all sinking or starving
While they wait for the right price to chart in
Their spreadsheets
But we're not just dead meat
Not yet. We're not beat
Don't tell Mama, I don't want to worry her

But Grandad, why didn't people act earlier?

Dear Gracie,
I'm sad I won't see you for a while
But I'm glad you're being a brave girl
Getting regular food has been a trial
Some of the farmers' crops have started to fail
They say the soil
Has lost its nutrients
But our president
Has promised residents
That the threat against
The food and water supply
Will be contained
And won't be allowed to run dry
As long as we all try
Not to take more than our share
As the police will make arrests, beware
And take care
Of each other

So Gracie, how's your mother?
And little brother?
Not so little now I bet!
And I'm sorry, pet
Our lot should have done more
After all, we had the evidence years before
We did not have the right governance for sure
And we liked our 4x4s

And holidays to foreign shores
And to eat strawberries
In January
I'm truly sorry, baby
We preferred to wait for techno fixes
So we could defer any meaningful shifts

But all too soon Europe was burning
Africa was starving
Asia was flooding
And America was fighting
It was really frightening
We thought this crisis would bite after we'd
lived
But it didn't. It's now.
For which I wish you will one day forgive
I hope you can understand
All my love,
Grandad

Dear Maths

Dear Maths,
I'm sorry there are only a few
Folks that don't think they're rubbish at you
Those that say they suck at Maths
Tough luck, they're multitude, it's true
Why does the government make
Teenagers suffer for the sake
Of ratios and rates of change
Geometry, circle theory
which makes them deranged
Maths teachers are thin on the ground
The decent ones don't stick around
I was lucky myself
My teacher was great, so in year 12
I studied maths and further maths
Which I managed to pass
With top marks
So off to study you at uni I went, it was a laugh
I had two friends who kept me on the right path
Even though I drank and got high
I never did sacrifice
My earnest drive to derive
The most elegant proofs
I particularly liked
Applied mathematics

Quantum mechanics
And some of those old classics
Maybe I should have studied physics
Worked in a lab where there were no limits
Searching for a unifying theory of everything
Marrying electromagnetism and gravity
But then I probably wouldn't be
A poet instead I'd be writing a poetry of sorts
In equations on chalkboards
I'm probably doing just that somewhere
In an alternative universe out there
Dearest Maths you were my first love
I'm sorry I've forgotten
So much of you, because
I've never needed to remember
The proof required for Schrodinger
Maybe one day in my later years
I'll relearn you before my brain disappears

Dreaming

Have you ever been awake
while you are dreaming?
Where your mind concocts plots
and is scheming
To keep you a prisoner where there are no bars
to prevent you leaving
Just tales that appear so real you don't question
The fantasy pieced together from your favourite
science fiction
Last time I was up all night
Making speeches, rehearsing the fight
The scenes replayed over and over
While the story required me
to stand stiff as a soldier
As I fell into a black hole
My atoms ripped apart
Where does go my soul?
I form a straight line from my head to my heart
The gravity turns up to infinity
While my parents make a call
To begin my journey back to reality
It's hard to leave the dream
I struggle, kick and scream
I've forgotten who I really am
I'm not an earth saving hero

I'm merely an ordinary woman
Needing a big injection and time
To bring me back down to zero

Lithium

How can this saltiest of salts
Be responsible for lifting me up
Up, up and out of the fault-
Lines, where I'm too high, I'm lost
Or so low, too low, I lose trust

But I'm now flying smooth for the long haul
Leaving behind my astronauts and ghosts
I hope I can cope without
The sea of my latest episode
Instead walk tall, and not stall
Despite all that I can recall
Of their intricate source code

Now I'm not certain
If this feeling I'm feeling
Is it because I've been moving?
Or is it because
My brain now has
Found a new position
Where much has been forgiven?

I'm cautious to say
It's now okay
No really okay

Come close, I'll whisper it
But don't tell my sister this
I think what I feel is
A strange, once forgotten sensation... happiness

Wednesday 4th October 2023

One thousand seven hundred and eleven days
since my last drink
Which means it's been one thousand seven
hundred and ten days
Since my last hangover
Where I woke up
Head fucked
Memory hazy
Piece together like a crazy
Time traveller
The previous night's activities
Must have gone against my proclivities

Five hundred and eighty one days since I left the
psyche ward
Blinking, dazed
Still a little crazed
Amazed at my new freedom
After a month banged up with some random
from Sweden
And a woman who sang along
To every single Beatles song
All day long
Out of tune
At full volume

One hundred and fifteen days
since my last psychosis
Floating off into a waking dream
Everything seemed hyper real and extreme
With my diagnosis
Not an ideal prognosis
20 times more likely to die by suicide
And expected lifespan
10 years less than the average man

Sixty three days since I last had sex
A Wednesday morning
Of what would be a new dawn in
A relationship
After all you called me your girlfriend
pretty quick
So when a few days later
You turned traitor
Claimed you were too broken
For this, whatever this is
So I took my tokens
And spent them on totems
To turn my almost hurt into poems

It's been three days since my last kiss
It started with a touch on my hip
In a club, not dancing to 90s rock music
I stood closer after that

And then you wrapped
Your arm around my back
I held your hand
And we continued to stand
Watching the mosh pit
Then you faced me and we kissed
I liked it
It reminded me of what I had missed

Queer

People often ask 'how do you identify'?
Not that it's any of your business but I
Would say queer not bi
As bi implies only women and men need apply
Actually what about those who are non-binary?
I find them hot also
Gender non-conforming
Scars on torsos
What matters more so
Is not what's in their pants
But what's in their heads and hearts, thanks

I've heard it all before though
'You're so greedy' or
'Pick a team'
I'm mean, really?
Or they say
You must be gay
But your own internalised homophobia is
preventing you from fully embracing your true
gay ways
And I say
'Er, no'
Anyway
I've got other dragons to slay

Like why am I still single?
Despite all and sundry apparently being
available
You would think
That if all genders are on the table
I'd be more able
To find someone, anyone
With which to have a little fun
Of the bedroom variety
Who also quietens my anxiety
And respects my sobriety
And is 100% okay
With helping change the duvet
Surely the loneliest of tasks
Not a lot to ask
A person to hold my hand
And fan
The flames of my creativity
And who I'll fancy and they fancy me
Just putting that out to the universe
Hello God, do you hear me?

Ocean

With three quarters
Of our planet covered in water
Don't you think Planet Earth oughta
Be called Planet Ocean?
The oceans are in perpetual motion
Moved by the moon, the wind, and when our
globe spins
Some of these currents
Take a thousand years
To journey round the world just once
While I marvel at this watery rock we live on
I prefer to stay on
Dry land
I'll happily sit on sand
Toes or a hand can be dipped in the water
But I'll go no further
Blame Spielberg
Or worse, John Williams
Surely millions
Of innocents too scared to go in to swim
Such simple elements
Da-duh, da-duh, da-duh, da-duh
Good God the
Terror evoked by those two notes
If I do end up swimming

I keep on looking
Peering through the gloom
Acutely aware the sea is somebody else's home

I also saw a poor man drown
On holiday, he was pulled out grey not brown
My father ran
He sprinted down the beach
Grabbed me tight and
He looked so frightened
So yeah you could say
Me and the sea
Don't agree
Girl's got issues
An invitation to swim I'll nearly always refuse

Running

I hate running
I've never found it fun in
Sunny weather or raining
Never got past the pain
Into the hallowed arena of endorphins
The brain drug that hooks you and forces
Mile after mile
Dressed in expensive lycra while
Hours tick by
Nike run club tries
To convince me to strap my trainers on
And take a little jog, hon
'Just 20 more minutes, you've got this'
The annoying American trainer insists
Assuming your run is utter bliss
Instead I'm falling into the abyss
I tell myself running is cheap
But when my lungs start to bleed
I really must concede
My trainers are gathering dust
My body reacts to running with disgust
Walking is much better, it says
Unhurried, calming and pain free instead

Born in August

You would have been born in August
The truth of this the rawest
Hello little lion
Pretend it's fine
But inside
Emptied
A void, please
No dwelling on what's been
We're done
No reruns
No time machines
And if they did exist
She'd go back to November
Attempt to resist
And drink less wine
So no lion
Would ever live
Inside
For that lonely night in December
Never, never
Least said about that the better
How's your pact with God going?
Blood keeps flowing
Clock keeps ticking
Tick tock

Tick tock
Tick tock
Too late
Fuck

Child Free

Free to lie in til half past three
Free to take off with a bag just for me
Free to buy a yellow velvet sofa
Free to invite them round to get closer

Free from creeping, sinking nauseousness
Free from pressure building, skin stretching,
trousers tightness
Free from aching breasts, prepping for the
mouth they soon will meet
Free from donating my body to a thief

Free from little sticky fingers making a mess
Free from answering inane questions
with a guess
Free from adverts assuming I'm a mum
Free from planning ahead
like a military operation

Free from school playground chat
Free from all that competitive crap
Free from peels of laughter
Free from seeing my face on another
Free from marvelling at amateur creations
Free from 24 / 7 dedication

Free from tiny heads that smell like home
Free from fists holding on tight to my thumb
Free from being the only one
to comfort crying creatures
Free from witnessing growth spurts and
maturing features

Free from constant worrying
Free from underwear borrowing
Free from teenage self harm and smoking
Free from red eyes and joint toking

Free from being a single identity of 'mother'
Free to be the dam so their shit goes no further
Free to regret that thing I did all over again
Free to grieve a pain that I'll never give a name

Anaesthesia

She watches the bubbles rise to the top
Forgetting her craving, unable to stop
Impatient and thirsty for the first sip
The warmth as it spreads
The panic that dips

She doesn't care for the taste,
she needs the relief
Effective anaesthetic, by the forth or the fifth
Friction that burns, just by existing
Is soothed by the salve and mistaken belief

She drinks
And she drinks
And she drinks
And she drinks
And when she comes to
Only then does she think

What the hell happened?
Who did she attack?
How did she get here?
To this bed in this flat?
Who is beside her?
This young brown-haired man

To piece it together
With no clues and no plan

Her head begins pounding
To a 4-4 kick drum
Which is nothing compared
To the shame that will come
As she picks up her clothing
And creeps out the door
Full of self-loathing
Regret and remorse
Making earnest pledges she intends to keep
Only to break them at the first bottle she meets

Her single solution
To this rot in her soul
Is to drown it in liquid
Lose all sense of control
Obliterate herself
And wipe her memory clean
Find more bubbles rising
Awaken thirst in her genes

Until one morning she feels it
The path as it forks
With a brimful of dread
An unknowable force
Asks with a whisper
Are you done now? Because

What's next is a choice
Between the end or a pause
Where you go to a room
Full of stories like yours

She feels a special kinship
With these fellow drunks
She asks one of them to help her
Her heart's so loud it thumps
As she dries out and defrosts
She realises what she wants
Is to feel the sunlight on her face
And her spirit free for once

Body

Fat
Large
Lardy
Heavy
Chunky
Curvy
Not how I should talk to my body
Even though I can feel quite blobby
I've grown some thighs
That could rival
Beyonce or Amy Schumer
I'm desperate that my future
Body will be smaller
I never used to care
I could wear
Anything a size ten
No dieting
No calorie counting
I'd be slim
Lean
Skinny
Slender
Even after a three day bender
I'd stick at eight stone eleven
Still able to visit carbohydrate heaven

I lazily practised yoga
Only because it lowered
Stress not to alter how I dressed
Things are messed up
Since quetiapine has intervened
Causing me to snooze until noon
And crave more and more food
Especially the sugary kind
My stomach lags behind my mind
Over the last year I've grown
Gained at least two stone
Spread out on my belly, bum and hips
Because of all the crap that's passed my lips
But I have to take the hit
There's not a choice between
Skinny and crazy
Or chubby and sane
I could probably lose the weight
With zero carbs for three months straight
Or I'll have to get used to
Being balanced, happy and less rude to
My body, it's doing its best
I just wish it would weight a little less

Woman

Long hair
Vacant stare
Curvy hips
Big tits
Tiny waist
Delicate face
Gapped thighs
So many lies
Society
Patriarchy
Magazines and TV
That boy from school called Christopher Lee
They all want us to believe
Want us to be
And how can we?

Our flesh
Is valued by inches
We're just a guest
In their world we're bitches
On a level with dogs
Go do the dishes
Burn all the witches

Born from Adam's rib
Responsible for the first sin
Periods are unclean
No touching
No property owning
No voting

Weinstein
David Blaine
Louis CK
Kevin Spacey
James Franco
Mario Testino
Chris Brown
And now Russell Brand
They are just the tip of the fucking iceberg
Thousands of arseholes we instinctively give a
wide berth

We teach our girls to
Never talk to strangers
Carry our keys in between our fingers
Text our friends when we're safe at home
Never, ever walk down a dark street alone
Why aren't we teaching our boys
That girls are not toys
Our bodies not their property
Even for their eyes to gaze upon hungrily

What kind of world is it when we have to rely
upon Barbie
To show a generation of kids what feminism
might be

Meanwhile we are called
Bossy
Bitchy
Bubbly
Sassy
Hysterical
Irrational
Emotional
Loud
Barren
Slut
Frigid
Prude
Or just plain rude

I'm tired of walking the line between
Pretty but not threatening
Thin but not too thin
Ambitious but not aggressive
Compliant when it's really oppressive

Is it just me or do you hate the word 'actress'?
I especially detest it when they call the English
football team "The Lionesses"

Makes their victories sound so pathetic
Is a female doctor called a doctress?
Or a plumberess?
A builderess?
An accountantess?
A solicitoress?
What utter fucking nonsense

Maybe one day
We'll be able to say
People are now equal
Although it's less of a challenge
To redress this imbalance
And use our talents
To invent
An equal amount of gendered put downs for
men
And see how much they like it then

Cillian Murphy's Face

If I were to one day wake up to that face
That exquisite face
A canvas of perfection and grace
To gaze, unfazed in the clearest of ways
Straight into his bright ocean blue eyes
I think I would be happy to die
Or at least cry
Cry big fat tears of delight and try
To not scream, "holy shit, is this a dream?" and
then cream
My underwear, although I hope they'd be long
gone over there
Discarded on the carpet
I'd have shaved my armpits
Just in case, oh good gracious me, that face

There must be a hundred men
Condemned to be ugly
Their mugs free to live in anonymity
Just for this one face
To use all the available beauty
In the vicinity

I confess
I think I like his face best

When it's a mess
Covered in mud and blood or when his fist goes
thud
As Jim, from that grim 28 days later zombie film
Or when he lights a fag and takes a drag
As Tommy Shelby, voice low where he might
well be
The most beautiful Brummie

You know he's actually quite funny
When interviewed next to
Jamie Dornan or Christopher Nolan
Ordinarily shy but professionally this guy
Is well into his craft
His laughs are seldom heard
But get past the fourth or third drink
And I'm sure he'd think
"Fuck it, let's go
After all I've played a hero"
Of sorts, the Father of the bomb
And yes his time has come
To win an Oscar
Because there
In those many close ups
The IMAX camera shows us
His eyes that shine bright blue
Even in black and white, through
Interrogations and investigations
His beauty never fades

When Albert Einstein waves
I saw that film three times
If I ever met him I'd not be fine
I'd attempt to play it cool
But he's no fool

I bet if we ever had sex
He would certainly, selflessly
Make me come, two, no three
Times before he stared at me and said "hey hon
You're beautiful and my kind of fun"
And then I'd be done
I most definitely would cry
Before I died
To reply into those eyes as if I had won…
The ultimate prize to say 'I love you, Cillian'